ISBN   1 85534 589 7

Printed and bound in Great Britain.

Rapunzel

Retold by Judy Hamilton
Illustrated by Lindsay Duff

Tarantula Books

Once there lived a poor craftsman and his wife. After waiting many years, they found that the craftsman's wife was expecting a baby and they were overjoyed. The craftsman tried to look after his wife, but they were very poor and sometimes very hungry. One night, in desperation, the craftsman went to steal some vegetables from a nearby garden, but he was caught by the wicked witch who owned the garden. He begged her for mercy.

"My wife is going to have a baby," he said, "and she needs proper food!"

The witch was heartless.

"You may take the vegetables," she said, "but when the baby is born, it shall be mine!"

The craftsman and his wife were very frightened. After some weeks, the baby was born, a beautiful little girl, and they named her Rapunzel. They tried to get on with their lives and forget about the witch.

But the witch had not forgotten about them. One night, just after they had tucked Rapunzel into her cot and rocked her to sleep, the witch appeared. Again the craftsman begged her for mercy, but the witch paid no attention to his pleas. In a flash of blue smoke, she took the baby and disappeared from sight.

The craftsman and his wife never saw their beloved daughter again.

The witch was determined to keep Rapunzel all to herself. She built a tall tower in the middle of a very deep forest and kept the child there. Nobody was allowed to see Rapunzel. As Rapunzel grew, the witch would never let her cut her hair. When Rapunzel was old enough to become curious about the world outside, the witch blocked up the door at the foot of the tower, so that Rapunzel could not get out. When the witch came to see Rapunzel, she would call up to the tiny window, high up in the tower:

"Rapunzel, Rapunzel, let down your hair!"

Then Rapunzel would let her hair fall down out of the window, and the witch would take hold of it and use it like a rope to climb up into the tower.

Poor Rapunzel. The witch gave her clothes and plenty to eat, but she left her alone in the tower most of the time. Rapunzel longed for someone to talk to, and for a chance to explore the forest and the world beyond. She had a lonely life. She would spend her days looking out of the window and dreaming. Sometimes she would sing songs that she had made up herself. Her voice was strong and clear, but the songs that she sang were always sad.

One day, a prince was riding in the forest and caught the sound of Rapunzel's singing on the wind through the trees. He was entranced.

"What a beautiful, sad song!" he said. "I must find the lady who sings so sweetly and so sadly!"

The prince urged his horse on through the trees in the direction from which the sound of singing was coming. As he got nearer, the sound grew sweeter and clearer. Then, all of a sudden, it stopped and the prince heard another voice, not sweet and clear like the first, but creaking and rasping. The voice was saying:

"Rapunzel, Rapunzel, let down your hair!"

At that point, the prince's horse moved within sight of the lonely tower, and he saw a beautiful girl let a long mane of shining golden hair out of the topmost window. Then he saw a gnarled and wrinkled old woman climb up the girl's hair and in through the window.

Determined to find out more about the beautiful girl with the lovely voice, the prince waited until the witch climbed down from the window and disappeared from sight in the forest. Then he walked up to the foot of the tower and called out softly:

"Rapunzel, Rapunzel, let down your hair!"

Just as she had done when the witch had called to her, the girl let her long, golden tresses fall from the window, and the prince climbed up.

Rapunzel was very surprised to see the prince climbing up towards her, but he assured her that he meant her no harm. She let him in through the window of the tower and told him how the witch kept her a prisoner.

The prince stayed and talked to Rapunzel for a very long time. Long before he left the tower, he realised that he had fallen in love with her. He promised that he would come back and see her as soon as he could. Rapunzel was delighted to have found a friend to talk to at last. As time went on, she realised that life without the prince would be unbearable. One day, when the prince came to visit, she told him:

"I cannot stay locked in this tower for ever. I need your help to escape."

The prince gladly agreed to help Rapunzel, and the next time he visited, he brought a skein of strong silk thread. Rapunzel began to weave a ladder to escape from the tower.

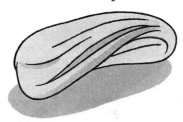

Every evening, the prince came to the tower and each time he came he brought more silk for Rapunzel. The ladder was soon nearly long enough for Rapunzel to climb down from the tower. Rapunzel did her best to keep her secret from the witch, and always worked on her weaving at night when she was alone. During the daytime she kept the ladder well hidden in case the witch came to visit her.

But one day, the witch did not come at her usual time. She was later than usual, and when she called up to Rapunzel, Rapunzel thought it was the prince. She let down her hair, calling:

"Hurry, my darling, I have been so lonely without you today!"

The witch was furious when she heard this and realised that Rapunzel had been seeing someone behind her back. She climbed into the tower, demanding to know who it was. Rapunzel, although she was terrified, would not give in and tell the witch. The witch flew into a rage and, taking a pair of scissors from her pocket, cut off Rapunzel's beautiful golden hair. Then she cast a spell to make Rapunzel vanish from the tower and land far away, in the wilderness. It was a place where she could wander forever, lost and alone. It was a cruel punishment.

When this was done, the witch waited in the tower for the prince to arrive.

Some time later, the prince rode up to the tower and called as usual:

"Rapunzel, Rapunzel, let down your hair."

He had no idea that the witch was in the tower. The witch dangled Rapunzel's hair out of the window. Eager to see his beloved Rapunzel, the prince climbed up the hair at great speed. But as he climbed in at the window, it was not Rapunzel waiting to see him, but the witch, her face almost purple with fury.

"So you think that you can take my Rapunzel away from me, do you?" the witch screamed. "Let me tell you, I am too clever for you! Rapunzel has gone, so far from here that you will never find her again!"

The witch threw the prince from the window and he fell to the ground, landing in a thorn bush. The thorns pierced his eyes and blinded him. He staggered into the forest, unable to see where he was going, but too full of sorrow to care. The witch cackled with fury.

The prince wandered on, mile after mile through the countryside, in search of his dear Rapunzel. He could not bear to think that he had lost her forever. Everywhere he went, he called her name in the vain hope that she might be nearby and hear him and answer him. It was many years later when the prince wandered into the wild country, where, unknown to him, the witch had banished Rapunzel.

On and on the prince walked, calling for Rapunzel. Then one day he caught the sound of singing on the wind; the same sweet songs and clear voice that he had heard so long ago.

"Rapunzel!" he called. "Have I found you at last?"

Rapunzel heard him and answered:

"Yes, my darling prince! You have found me!" and she ran to him, weeping with joy.

As she embraced the prince, Rapunzel's tears fell into his eyes. Miraculously, the prince found that he could see again. Rapunzel and the prince knew that they would never again be parted. They returned to the prince's kingdom together, and there they lived in happiness for the rest of their lives.